M000211454

Spellbound

Spellbound

Sara Miller

Winner of the 2016 Burnside Review Press Book Award
Selected by Ada Limón

Burnside Review Press   Portland, Oregon

Spellbound
© 2018 Sara Miller

All rights reserved

Cover Image: from U.S.P.R.R. Explorations & Surveys,
47th Parallel, Birds – Plate XXIV, circa 1859

Cover Design: Susie Steele
Layout: Zach Grow

Printed in the U.S.A.
First Edition, 2018
ISBN: 978-0-9992649-2-8

Burnside Review Press
Portland, Oregon
www.burnsidereview.org

Burnside Review Press titles are available for purchase from the
publisher and Small Press Distribution (www.spdbooks.org).

for Bill and Marguerite

The Art of Detection   13

Parable in a Meadow   14

Countermeasures   15

Cairo   16

Gone to the Devil   17

Destiny of Species   18

His Mark   19

Too Late   20

The Yellow Emperor   21

Parable in a Dark Age   25

Asides on the Barometer   26

Moves in the Field   27

Lunch   28

Just Sayin'   29

Be Passersby   31

Blink   33

Overtaken   34

Vigil   35

New Year's Eve   36

Parable in a Book   41

The Consolation   43

Bodily   45

Episode   46

Locutions   47

Meditation with Microscope   48

Spellbound   49

It Comes to Grief   51

Gravitas   52

Parable for Inclement Times   57
It Came to Me   58
Roots   60
Reckoning   61
Plot Twist   62
The Lobster Bride   63
Bible Study   65
The Sum of the Insignificant   67
Nocturne   69
Revelations   70

Acknowledgments   72

The Art of Detection

I took the possum apart by myself.
There were no instruments, per se;
mostly it was questions, telepathy.
But these were enough.

They revealed that the middle of the possum
and the middle of the night are one and the same.
The night is all that is in him.
It is how he goes, how he secretly lives.
It is what he is hiding.

Now it is no mere dream of the night
that occupies the possum, nor revelations
in the night, nor expectations of day
begotten by night, nor any yearnings
or conjurings thereof—just night,
the blackness and breathing.

There is nothing to be done, of course.
Night is uncorrectable.
And I am not now, nor have I ever been,
a healer. I just go into the woods.
Then I go deeper.

PARABLE IN A MEADOW

I consider the field
and in it the tree.
"What is the tree made of,"

I ask the finches, but they are
busy scolding something.
Squirrel's stereo is too loud, naturally.

Finches want peace and quiet,
squirrel and his fraternity
want to party late into the evening.

The beautiful evening
in her periwinkle cocktail dress
against which everything is leaning.

The sky, the lusty owl, the paper
lanterns—even the music, which
some love and some hate.

"That's what the tree is made of,"
says an old worm, passing by.
"Good and evil. Also—evil and good."

COUNTERMEASURES

I wish I could keep my thoughts in order
and my ducks in a row.
I wish I could keep my ducks in a thought
or my thoughts in a duck.
My point is that we all exist, wetly, in the hunt.
The ducks are aware of this
in their own way, which is floating.
The way of the mind is brevity.
There may be other thoughts on other days
in the minds of other and better men
and their constant companions, the women,
but these same tidy capsules—never.
This is just one of the things
I noticed about my thoughts
as they passed easefully by.

Cairo

The evidence was in and it went to the contrary.
The contrary wound around us rather like a river.
The river reacted, spiderlike, tangling up its legs
with other wet parts we thought we knew,
such as creeks and fjords and deltas and such.

A beaver sits on the riverbank watching all of this unfold.
He doesn't know what a fjord is, and he doesn't care
for other waters, or even other beavers, or the merest
hint of other business, so he removes this evidence.

Then he builds a structure which for years he is rehabbing.
Inside it is hollow and there is his nest.
He is a dark little bastard, all the same.
The water had a fine way of being, now it is tortured
by these nests and their vassal.

Yet the river doesn't overthrow the beaver.
Quite the contrary. The river goes around polite as a snake.
It argues a tiny bit at the edges of the lodge,
where young beavers could be napping.

You and I would let loose a flood of tears. Not the river.
You and I would seep hotly into our darkest places,
but not the river. It is a long way from home
and has that on its mind. The day of rising,
when the temples will all be cleansed
and the whole unfathomable truth will out.

According to the waters. According to their book.

GONE TO THE DEVIL

Some gulls are arguing over a tea bag.
It was lying in the sand
when one of them speared it.
Another came in shrieking and pointing,
a menace, whose envy was transparent.
He couldn't have cared less for the soggy
packet until he glimpsed it dangling
from his rival's mouth.
Cherchez la femme, as they say....

And so in this fashion I concocted
various plots for the bickering birds.
I dressed them colorfully. I gave them
mannered lines and a genealogy
like the kings of England.
All to avoid the vexing and unanswerable
question of why they exist at all,
walking about on their legs,
blessing and cursing the little sailboats,
dogged and insatiable like the great moths
but above even these.

The kings of England!
The wars! The tea!
Oh, it is hopeless....

DESTINY OF SPECIES

A sign appears in the forest
which has no use for signs.

Spores and torrents,
these are its wants.

These and dusk, which
at last folds the birds

into its pleats.
We've no idea

how the trees endure;
what they're thinking up there

in the avian belt.
All that melody, perfidy.

The to and fro of fledglings
on their way to death.

Today singing, tomorrow
quenched like a wick.

I hate the sign
and do what it says.

His Mark

The chameleon would not touch the marriage.
His property he kept in his teal head.
What he wanted was to recover
his vanishables. He could not.

A private ocean occurs to him. He looks down
at it from his precipice and makes a phony
gesture there about his life, about all life.
He deserved to be dealt out of the world, he thought.
He was loath to start anything here, he thought.
The sun no longer pleased him or convinced him.
He had had sex but it withstood him.
He had eaten but it was small.
He was tired of concoctions and dread.
It seemed a mistake had been made,
everywhere, and he no longer felt the all.

He managed to pack this and more
into the one gesture. It was brief and exact.
It had the element of surprise and almost
surprised him, or at least the woman in him,
who was about to disappear herself
when the complete male human laughter
returned, with its boat, its sanderlings,
its alibi net, and its lock, the one for the top
of the world, and also for the bottom.

Too Late

Nevertheless, I glance outside.
Four cats patrol the courtyard,
each his own quadrant,
established long ago.

They haven't seen me.
I draw the curtains nonetheless,
a freshman mistake, for now
it was dark and there is nothing
to be drawn against that.

Night within, cats without.
A phrase comes to me from a book—
"Immanent dualism," a character's last aside.
What troubled his courtyard,
I'd like to know.

Sunshine, I should think,
would scatter those cats.
On second thought—
how imminent?

The Yellow Emperor

The crime of disappointment
does not exist among the crickets.
I asked them today as I strolled through their meadow.
I spread my arms wide to express it, desire.
I explained folly and fortune
as I have known them and stood between them,
the difference being—a blade of grass.
I spoke of Jupiter and its long year,
and Ecclesiastes, a sage, who loathed
all hours equally and in turn.
I played a great chord in E
with my hands on the loamy earth
to impart my meaning better, like Beethoven.
I did not leave out the Magdalene, who was clinging,
nor the ambush of the Americas in their sleep,
nor Chuang Tzu and his meeting with the skull,
that uncontrite fossil, that happy head,
and I lowered my voice, as at a bedside.
Is there any such thing? I cried softly.
And they answered me in full alarm:
The bee! The bee! The bee!

Parable in a Dark Age

The minnow opened his mouth and began to speak.
His words flew at me from the ninth century.
The ninth century!
Troglodytes shuffled through the hazel.
Their lanterns revealed them
and the branches shrank back in alarm.
"But they too vanished in the history of England,"
burbled the minnow, as one gill breathed deeply
and his eyes bore into mine.

Then last night, around two, in a dream,
Jess bought a loft in West Town.
On the ground floor, improbably.
In fact it was only a carport with a retractable
roof, large enough for twelve sedans.
We all looked on admiringly as Jess
maneuvered the roof back and forth
to show us how the twelve would fit,
head to tail like layered fish.

"And yet," interrupted my minnow,
"There really weren't any cars, were there?"

And for a moment I was fooled.
Then I was redeemed.
Then I stopped talking into that stream forever.

Made it through the morning in pieces.
Blame, fuss appeared. Did I summon them?
I have so little to do, like a voluptuary,
angling around the apartment, barking
approval at this, cursing that.

In the bath I discover Greenland.
It is not so large. But the people living there,
how inevitable their philosophy is.
"Death is always mistaken for someone else."
"Truth ruins a landscape."
"One cat is a warning; two are destiny."
"Life looks small on the ocean; it is just the tip."

I could have been many things to many people.
The bargains and arrangements around love
could have been made. Some were, in fact.

Now my glass enjoys my company.
Here we are, padding over to the window
where the sun is pouring in,
meaning to close the blinds because
it looks hot out, not that it is hot.

MOVES IN THE FIELD

Had to come in out of the people.
They blew me about so.
Was told of the life taking place
elsewhere. Went to check on that,
flying late and low over the west.

Saw no house, no shade.
Sat down on the damp bank
of the far shore at the left
edge of the world, against which
the sea endlessly lapped.

So now there were two of us,
who beat the world by day
and caressed it by night and
the world didn't say yea
and she didn't say nay.

LUNCH

So much for wonderment, said Frank,
as the watery drinks arrived.
Which is more tired and worn,
asked Mary, life or death?
We smoked, and thought this over.
Frank had business in Detroit.
Mary had a class she thought would save her.
Lou was moving amphibiously through
his day, and now a square of sunlight
suggested that he hurry it along.

I had nothing, was expected nowhere,
and so stayed to consider the snowy owl.
I thought of its quiet breast and its grave eye.
I considered the backward head, short and necessary.
I thought of it in lamplight, then in moonlight.
I believe I whispered to its left wingtip.
I could have done more, but I didn't.
I left it at that, according to my nature,
which used to wonder about many things
and now merely wonders about them all.

Just Sayin'

One outsized testicle is conversing
with another outsized testicle
about the things that interest them.

This is awkward, as it is not my habit
to surveille the male parts unless
and until—they are discussing me.

But you know how it accidentally is,
to stumble upon a pair of hobos
under their oak, where they are quarreling

mildly in that entertaining fashion
for which bourbon was invented, after which,
they look up at the sky and are silent.

The testicles have their peace. I have mine.
Who wins, and for how long, and to what end
are questions the mind can't answer,

nor can the body. How, then, they should
come to us as questions at all—that too
is unexplained and lives in gangways.

By now it will be clear that what I'm trying
to tell you has not been disclosed to me,
nor would I wish to repeat, in mixed company,

all I know. Not that it's a contest, in which
one of the duelists pretends to have missed
while the other appears to be dead.

BE PASSERSBY

Awakened in the early hours
to provide an assessment of my life

I found I had no remark.
There was simply nothing to say.

But how can that be, pursued
my interlocutor, a tireless hound.

It can be, I replied, just as any
afternoon can be on which you are

strolling among a grove of locusts
admiring their great trunks

and innocently overturn a stone
under which lies a solitary skink.

For a moment you regard one
another (human!...skink!)

though what the skink's thoughts
about it are you do not entertain

for yours are bubbling. What is his length
and his weight? What are his habits and troubles?

What is his dreamwork? His ambition? His remorse?
He utters a fearful peep and vanishes,

leaving you somewhat taken aback
given that you meant no harm,

were merely curious, an unintentional
man on his gentlest of wanders

among the last, late boudoirs not yet
encumbered by decorum or hopelessly

nettled by do-not-disturb signs, unless,
of course, you count the stone.

BLINK

Empires come and go. Rice lasts.
What had it to do but stay
as the hooves and ages crept past?

Occasionally a leaf blows in—company
at last—or the refugee on squishy feet
tells all he knows to the listening ear.

Rice is not impressed. To stay
put, endure, and be believed
or move in bodies and ideas

like the flying, warring men?
Rice has time to consider
all this and is lonelier still.

Night falls, solving some things,
but not the restless, rootless men.
Even Moon in her starry field

is speechless, the awful mouth
agape for what appears, in rice
years, an eternity.

Overtaken

Parallelogram dropped its sides.
Who sweet-talked it into this is beside
the point—the point is now settled,
the door is open, and soft-bodied mice
rush in, it is their time.

Yesterday it steamed homeward,
two washed Dobermans under its eaves.
Today the papers are full of unfoldings.
Another box is lowered.

Nobody can make head or tail
of time passing, the manifests
waiting to be written.
A Normandy miss develops a polyp,
boy soldiers won't sprout again.
By the chapel a small party
gathers as if nothing previously
had plunged so low so successfully.

Tombstones tilt, towers fall;
an envelope of earth awaits us all.
Death sits on a windowsill
looking like a biscuit.
Never mind, say the mice,
Let's just go.

VIGIL

The neighborhood changed
the day the dead moved in.

The rich sold their homes.
The reputable fled.

Those of us who stayed
sat in our windows

watching the first carloads
pull up, trying to peer

into their faces.
It was beastly quiet.

One by one
a few of us went over

to see if there was anything
we could do.

But there was nothing
we could do.

New Year's Eve

In my thinking
about the universe
I've reached an impasse.

We were all in the kitchen
together, tossing around
ideas from a long time ago,
turning them over, humming.

I couldn't get past the opinion
that it's all a shame, and that
beyond shame doom itself
is rather passive, like a chorus

that doesn't come in for a while,
though the look on their faces
is telling, and makes the interim
loveless, inevitable, and cold.

I said this into my glass,
and the ice agreed
that it was so.

Parable in a Book

A mouse came in, briefly it breathed.
I was handling some papers

which caused them to whisper
and it seemed the mouse was listening.

Is one of us going to speak, I thought,
or will it dwindle into staring?

The hot eyes looked up imploringly,
a vote for staring.

It was evening when it happened with the mouse.
I was done with the television,

I'd fixed some troublesome verse.
A mathematical problem

not a musical one.
But no help from my poem

for the questioning mouse,
and none from the masters.

Not even Tolstoy.
I looked all through

The Kingdom of God Is Within You.
The mouse merely waited

while I read it to myself,
and then, inevitably, to him.

THE CONSOLATION

Once I was watching the sea.
I couldn't seem to get a break.

I thought the break would come
from there, but as I was watching it

I began to see beyond it,
and in the beyond was a room.

The octagonal, peach-tinted, parlor-
sized room containing the da Vinci.

The da Vinci lives modestly on a tree
trunk in the middle of the room.

It does not have doubloons
in its mouth or tattoos on its belly.

It is speechless, sinless, and cool.
People stroll up to it unawares

like fish to a hook and begin to peer
into it with their brown eyes,

their blue eyes, their grey-green eyes.
Whatever eyes they brought with them.

Whatever eyes they can find. Whatever
eyes are required to peer into a thing

like that if they are to see anything,
anything at all. But of course

they see everything. Life itself,
and the sea herself. The promenade

of days followed by the hangover
of nights, after which the days repeat,

and so on, insanely. At least it seems so
at the time. Later one remembers it

differently and is completely happy.
Later still one forgets entirely,

as in a dream, saying only,
"I was surrounded by Botticellis,

the Botticellis of renown,
each more beautiful than the last."

BODILY

I was thinking about the buttocks
because the artist has parked them here,

in the middle of the gallery where there's
no ignoring or getting around them,

despite some festive color gatherings
and trysts of foil and feathers on nearby walls,

not that I understand such fey elements—
Is that Harlequin, discussing private matters

with a rotifer, under moonlight?
I am neither for nor against these works

on paper, I'm trapped by the buttocks is all.
I'm looking back, I've fallen behind, it seems

I've lost a bet. No matter what Dr. Johnson
may say of the matter, nobody ogles his own;

ergo this plastic peach will have to do,
its two bloodless lobes tame as kittens.

On the other side is a face we don't see.
Because it is unbearable, our cadaver.

EPISODE

A Martian lands in a man's backyard
as a result of various mechanical
accidents in space. Now he lives
in the man's garage apartment,
tinkering and teaching,
his retractable antennae unobserved
by all save—well, save Bill Bixby,
the actor, now it can be told.

Later Bixby had another show
in which he fathered a human boy.
A small generation had passed by then,
yet somehow I was still watching.

Time speeds up, which is impossible,
for how could it? Now Bill Bixby is dead,
Uncle Martin, too, who may both
have taken real-life secrets to their graves.
Either no one asked them
or they forgot to speak up in time.

Time should not be allowed to accelerate.
It harms the planets.
It causes undue suffering on the green earth.
It silences the actors, good and bad,
and then it silences us.

Compared to this,
television is a nightingale.

LOCUTIONS

I found myself in the spine
of a little French dictionary,
which turned out to be roomier
than I'd thought, than anyone
had thought.

I languished in the early going,
under *abattoir* and *boulangerie*.
I drifted in a melancholy current
around *jusque* and *jamais*.
I performed a set of somersaults
in the eddies over *longtemps*.
I was at peace.

My friends would be
importantly engaged all day.
Back-to-back appendectomies,
yachting assignments, divorce.
I looked these up, they were
smaller than I'd thought.

Words change nothing
and yet we go on speaking them
as if a lifeboat might pop out
with our last breath,
but it never does.
Flowers come instead.

Alors. Eh bien.

MEDITATION WITH MICROSCOPE

The wish is lodged in the back of the eye.
No, the eye is back and the wish passes forth.
No, the wish is a tide in the eye that opens and closes.

A bead of sand, on its way to eternity, has come this far.
It is an object in a funny situation.
It does not look too deeply inside itself
nor too curiously around itself.
How will it be to meet in the meeting place?
You will not hear that from its lips.

A swimmer stands in the foam,
decisionless, but friendly.
Are there only elements
and what is best for them.
That is the question.

The answer is in that little fish, tucked in it.

SPELLBOUND

Two women on a train
sit beside me.
I am young and the world

is flying and I am watching.
One of them is frosty.
The other turns like a leaf

to hand me something—
it looked for all the world like a page.
I thought at the time

that it needed me and I was right.
The letters fell into place
and simple flowers grew.

Now it talks unceasingly
in long white verses,
as if at a wedding,

something women understand
and gently want and then regift.
I myself agree with Herbert,

who in a dark mood conjured
the mushrooms underfoot
unseen by bride or groom

and with him I say, Perhaps
the world is unimportant after all,
though this is not what one discusses

with women on a train,
no matter how long the journey
or untroubled the land.

IT COMES TO GRIEF

A fire in the lumber yard—none can save it.
The man racing near with his bucket is a blur.
They are both too late; they will never arrive.
It will come to grief.

The picayune face of the water in its pail.
It cannot control its trembling on this night mission,
which is preposterous. Its cup is round and holy,
but its tears will come to naught.

The woods look on, horribly, as they are next.
Yet they crowd closer with expressions rich as ours
and last forever. The sky is disinterested in a brown way.
It could help, but it won't. So it presides.

The salty flame alone cries out, completely stunned.
It can't stay where it loves. It can't be comforted
by any touch. There will always be darkness, it says.
The flame following thee rests its head. It can't be saved.
    So it burns.

GRAVITAS

The overweight, overnight parts
that came to me in a dream.

Their clothes no longer fit,
it was this that brought them

to me crying, their faces twitching.
That had to end. No, they said,

it didn't. So I rolled over to ghosts
that couldn't dent a pillow.

The clock shed. Night pulled its
burdens into harbor and I woke,

glad for the day, its flying minute,
its tell-tale light, that genie work,

and the everlasting perturbations
of my people, their glories,

their heavy last words.
And for these, I rose.

Parable for Inclement Times

Because a light rain was falling
I did not visit the possum in his little acreage.
I thought about him, though,
as I woke from a slight beer headache
to find myself deep inside the First Psalm,
where one murmurs God's law day and night.

Usually I lace my fingers through the fence.
That is what surrounds and imprisons him.
So it happens that I am the free one,
though this is not how it feels.

If the possum has a God and is murmuring
to him, I will not be there to witness it.
Only his log mansard and his leaf bed
will be any the wiser. Unless they are
the same God, in which case—

Ah. But surely you know all of that by now.

It Came to Me

We haven't seen the sun in weeks,
the sky is hateful, and the birds
who were fixed up once are returning
to Latin America.

One remains on my block, singing
for what it's worth. A grocer bird,
with a crisp, attractive apron and a bold voice
which I interviewed and which said:

"It's discouraging, to come so far for a thing
and lose it. I stayed on longer than most,
but for what? We're rotted through,
my wife won't lift her head.

"This was our only stake, you know—
above the petals and ponds, in the mammoth
arms of trees where light is everything...."
And he looked away.

"The earth will not reject anyone forever,"
I offered, but he shook himself, as if of dust.
"It's you who say it," he sang,
in five cold tones, and suddenly I realized

who and where I was, and what I was doing,
and what for, though I still didn't know why,
or for how long, and I still couldn't tell
the good from the merely outnumbered,
or the unlucky from the truly misbegotten,

though of course there are so many more
than these under the sun, it's just that these
are so insistent.

ROOTS

I stumble upon the definition of man.
I cough ceremoniously, I am unhurt.
The definition, on the other hand....

I embrace a leaf, then a folder.
The folder by default. It is tired
of my fondling, which is profitless.

No paper has emerged from it,
none gone in. There is little left
between us save mutual contempt.

That the Sphinx gives up nothing
does not prevent my shouting at it,
nor the shouts of man generally

at the statues, buildings, obelisks, and cliffs.
Waving his arms, coughing ceremoniously,
demanding his definition, certain that it will be big.

You see how it is with my days, nights.
I would pass compellingly into another age
if I could tear myself away.

God will fix it somehow, with his gypsies,
his castanets. Under the thrilling trees
of life, the trees of life....

RECKONING

I gathered around me all my selves.
Three pushed ahead with its scowl,
frightening the others.

Eight slept marvelously through
the hangover and into the various
necessary apologies subsequent to it.

Five worked without a net,
disguised as and finally betrayed by
Six, that motherless son.

But it was One, whom I liked,
wandering unchaperoned in her own mind
when the dachshunds trotted up.

They were miniatures, hardly innuendoes.
They clung to her lap like beetles, or dust.
She had to touch them to believe them.

"I will put them in a basket," she said
at last, and they gazed into her eyes.
The vaulted, immense blue sky
also looked in on the baby dogs.

"And I myself will carry the basket
when it appears before the Lord
and the Lord's favorites, the dead."

PLOT TWIST

I created little people
to populate the apartment.

I was in the process of standing
in socks—cradling a demitasse,

our lips were thinking of meeting—
I was in the business of assigning

parts, and began to see the village
take shape under the furniture

when someone rapped
mortally on the door.

My people looked up at me,
craning their necks,

whereupon it dawned
that this was no experiment

and I had no other choice
but to be good.

THE LOBSTER BRIDE

Sometimes I throw my arms out to the lake
in helpless misunderstanding and it does
the same. The waves come back to me
always, as I am pleasantly aware.

We are a little in love. It was the sun
who set us up when he withdrew
so quietly on his toes. You will say,
he did not withdraw, not withdraw.

But finally he did. And the women cried
about it. And the men abruptly sank
from their fisher faces on down.

I am full of misgivings and little wet
hopes. These ride ashore on the backs
of radiolarians, whose burden makes
them grieve and renders them speechless.

The news on Friday is not good.
Sunday seems too soon for singing
under one's breath, as if he might emerge
intact from the foam, a chivalrous mollusk

in his mollusk clippers, ready and roaring
to dine. For that is what it comes to,
my old water. My lovely watery dear.

My blue sand-petter. My fathom. My fellow.
My old Christian water and you two Buddhas
who have consented to live as my lips.

BIBLE STUDY

My dealings with the Pentateuch
coming to a close I glanced ahead,
picking and choosing.

Isaiah impressed me greatly
with his harrowing God, his wholesale
terror, and all those hearts turned inside out.

Bedouin erased. Incineration of tents.
Calamities beset even camels
as they lurched from one book to the next.

Above Jerusalem, a fit of curses spewed
for pages before God quieted himself
and settled into wooing the very desert

he had just destroyed. It is not the case
that good issues from evil, though
out of that smoking landscape,

footfalls on the ruined plain,
and a few verses on the whole earth
is singing, when moments before,

owls filled their houses. So back
I went through the ancient events,
men's flights and God's doings,

transcendent wisdom in chaste nuggets,
the major poetries of sex and sorrow,
kingly laments and hints of glories coming.

Great works all, but none greater
than the owls of Isaiah
in the houses of Israel—

breasts burning, eyes alight,
with the miraculous billet
that has befallen them.

The Sum of the Insignificant

Another molecule, this time deliberate
and in the act of forming water.
Why does it bother?

I consult the wind but learn little.
Usually I can count on its salient
asides—1989 would be just one example.

I was apprenticed to nature then,
or so I thought. I wrote of the lake:
"I can detect its immense thinking."

Just now a gull observes me
from his long face. A dune beetle
rights itself and proceeds, but to what end?

"It's been three years since Phil died,"
I complain to the sand. Ancient pause.
"Yes," they sigh at last. "We know all about it.

"But you lot are ever dire. Widows, the fatally
blemished, the driven to drink, all sons. And then,
in our condition, the troubles we've seen."

But I was distracted by a low speeding cumulus
darkening the waves running toward me.
"What turtles have you seen?" I mumbled dully,

but it was too late. Under the waves, celestial
night was emerging. The sun, at the moment of its glory,
sat fatly over Michigan like a pear on a plate.

And all the timber that once stood apart
now leaned together to form a shore
of surprising conviction. It was the kind

of moment one waits for all one's life,
taking one's life to unnatural places for,
until the life itself is strange and ablaze.

"Show me the way," I said, to the endlessness
of things. And lo, a great silvery compass
rose over us all, yes it did.

Nocturne

Last night in bed I mouthed
a prayer of my own composition.
It sounded offhand, it was carelessly
addressed, it twisted my meaning entirely,
it left an ache, I didn't know what I was doing.

So I took down my yellowed copy
of *French with Pictures*
by the late literary critic I. A. Richards
and I put my petition into soft French words.

I. A. Richards believed that irony
was the language of redemption.
He wrote and lectured famously on this,
but his masterpiece was *French with Pictures*.
"The chapeau is on the table."
"The man with the beard stands before the window."
"She comes from a village by the sea."

There is no improving the old traditions.
They are already mortal, partial, and wrong.
The woman at the table by the window
puts her head into her hands.
"Into your hands," she said.

Revelations

I know the walls of the castle will hold.
I know the wren is stronger than the wind.

I know the day of glory will begin and end
on time for everyone concerned.

Furthermore, I trust I will not emit
a spittle of curses and false ideas

on the street today. That my mouth
will not take it upon itself to act biblically

without permission. That I will not balk and bray
about evil like some ass from an old book.

That the shadows of the great buildings
will not rain their serpents and bees

down on my poor head again.
That I'll know where I'm going

with my nonsense and not the other way
around, and am able to keep walking,

exercising the lunacy to the point
of its exhaustion until it is a mere

arthritic thing no one notices, like a dog,
though not precisely a dog,

companionable nonetheless,
whom everybody forgets as they flee

the burning house but who is in fact
still in there, crying piteously

and earnestly and ceaselessly, though
in truth, he completely understands.

ACKNOWLEDGMENTS

Some of these poems originally appeared in the following journals:

America: "The Art of Detection"

First Things: "Vigil" and "The Sum of the Insignificant"

The Harlequin: "Destiny of Species," "Bodily," and "Meditation with Microscope"

Poetry: "Countermeasures," "Cairo," "Moves in the Field," "Spellbound," "Gravitas," and "Nocturne"

The Yale Review: "Gone to the Devil," "His Mark," and "The Yellow Emperor"

"Gone to the Devil" was reprinted in *Poetry Daily*.

"Spellbound" was reprinted in *The Hairpin*.

My thanks to the Fine Arts Work Center in Provincetown for its generous support during the completion of this book.

Sara Miller is the author of *Spellbound*, selected by Ada Limón as the winner of the 2016 Burnside Review Press Book Award. Her poems have appeared in *Poetry, The Yale Review, The Harlequin, Poetry Daily*, and elsewhere. She is a former poetry fellow of the Fine Arts Work Center in Provincetown and an alumna of the creative writing program at the University of Montana. She lives in Chicago.